MONROE PARK

S ONE of the most charming spots on either shore of Lake Michigan. Situated on the beach at South Haven, and close to the Black River, it is always the coolest and most pleasant of the resorts. It consists of a large piece of land, divided into lots, careful attention having been paid to landscape gardening, thus increasing the natural beauties of the site. On these lots there have been erected some **28 charming villas,** which are leased, **furnished,** for the season to those who desire to enjoy a **combination of country life and city comforts.** There are no inconveniences to put up with. Running water (from the city main), electric lights, and modern sanitary plumbing throughout the cottages, assure every comfort of a modern house. From beneath the windows, almost, Lake Michigan stretches away to meet the sky. For beauty, for comfort, for privacy in particular, there is no better place to spend your summer. For full particulars, address L. S. MONROE, Cashier First State Bank, SOUTH HAVEN, MICH.

Detail of promotional booklet, 1898

Published by the Historical Association of South Haven, Michigan
355 Hubbard Street, P.O. Box 552, South Haven, MI 49090

www.historyofsouthhaven.org

ISBN: 978-1537315676

Third Edition

Cottages and Resorts on the North Beach

Historic L. S. Monroe Park, South Haven, Michigan

1890-1960

By Helen B. O'Rourke
and Ken and Lynda Hogan

Sponsored by the Historical Association of South Haven, Michigan

SOUTH HAVEN, MICHIGAN, FURNISHED COTTAGES.

FOR SALE OR RENT.

ST. CLAIR—Seven rooms, gas, electric lights, city water, sewer, fire place, on the beach, nice wide porch, back porch inclosed, easy terms and price $1,500; will rent for season at $150. HEMENWAY, South Haven, Michigan.

GREEN COTTAGE—Seven rooms, bath, gas, electric lights, stone fire place, plaster and burlap finished, newly painted, large pleasant porches, city water, faces lake and park, extra well furnished, owned by a non-resident; for sale at $2,500; if not sold June 1st will rent for season at $250. HEMENWAY, South Haven, Michigan.

RED COTTAGE—Seven large rooms, toilet, bath and closets, large fire place, gas, electric lights, city water, sewer, fronts on beach and park; owned by St. Louis, Mo., party; who will sell at $2,750, on easy terms, or will rent for $275 season. HEMENWAY, South Haven, Michigan.

No.27—Six rooms, front and back porch, fine view of river, large lot, gas, electric lights, city water, sewer, newly papered

STONE LODGE—Ten rooms, pantry closets, two toilets, summer kitchen, large wood shed, big wide porch on three sides, built of rocks, finished in hardwood, oiled, has gas, electric lights, city water, sewer, large fire place, four lots, ½ block from paved street, one of the best built house in the section for sale to close estate for widow at $3,500; will rent for season at $350. HEMENWAY, South Haven, Mich.

FLORIDA—Twelve large rooms, gas, hot and cold water, electric lights, two toilet rooms, summer kitchen, two fire places, open stairway, hardwood finished, well painted, large wide porch on two sides with fine view of Lake Michigan, six lots only 100 feet to paved street, has been used as a private boarding house; is for sale on easy terms at $3,500; will rent if not sold by June 1st, at $350 completely furnished; a money maker for some one. HEMENWAY, South Haven, Michigan.

CUBBY Cottage—Six rooms, gas, electric lights, city water, sewer, paved street, good walks, winter construction, a year round home, large porch on two sides, price $1,200; terms easy; rent $125 for season. HEMENWAY, South Haven, Mich.

BEACH VIEW—Five rooms, fire place, electric lights, gas for cooking, located on the beach, large front porch, back porch, new, newly furnished; price $1,200; terms to suit; rent for season, $175. HEM-

Monroe Park, 1930s

Contents

Introduction

Preface to the 3rd Edition

In this edition, newly acquired images of original buildings are exchanged for photos of a later date. After the 1907 fire, modest one-story cottages and smaller resorts superseded many of the more ambitious structures. Presently, more extravagant styles are appearing once again.

A newly discovered 1902 panoramic photo which documents the early stage of Monroe Park's development is included. It was taken from the North pier and before the Avery street fire destroyed the Avery Beach Resort and many of those sizable cottages.

The idea for this picture book grew out of a feeling I had while producing the companion DVD, "Monroe Park."

Realizing that the DVD could not adequately embrace all the remarkable examples of vernacular architecture still standing or having disappeared since the end of the nineteenth century, I wanted to document them as thoroughly as possible.

Ken and Lynda Hogan, present owners of the duplex half of the 1898, "Florida Beach Resort" were indispensible researchers for this book. Together we perused the archival collections at the Historical Association of South Haven and the South Haven Memorial Library for early photographs, articles and advertisements. Two prominent photographic chroniclers of South Haven's history, R. W. Appleyard and Roy McCrimmon, were invaluable. Combing the tax records and city directories provided much information while The Sanborn Insurance Maps of the time gave great clues to where the early buildings stood or were moved about. Notes left by Jeanette Stieve and the support of James Ollgaard and the Historical Association of South Haven were absolutely vital.

The historical "L. S. Monroe Park Subdivision" is bounded by Avery Street, North Shore Drive, Lake Shore Drive and the Black river. Originally, the buildings had no address numbers and were identified only by the quaint names given by the owners. Later in the century, street numbers were assigned. The given map diagram uses the present day addresses to help serve as a tour guide through the region and includes adjacent areas significant to the resort trade. Demolition dates are noted.

In the 1960s, the resort and rental trade began a decline from its heyday and since then a different flavor has emerged with an emphasis on year-round and second home ownership. While summer rentals have persisted and a few restaurants lingered through the 1990s, the smaller resorts have vanished.

~Helen B. O'Rourke, 2016

The Beginnings

In the 1880s, L. S. Monroe, the son of pioneer Judge J. R. Monroe began the development of "Monroe Park" and formed The Monroe Park Association, which included most of the present day Monroe Park. One of the requirements of the Association was to sign a deed to include the following:

1. Premises to be used or occupied for residential purpose only; no business whatsoever.

2. No intoxicating liquors shall be sold or given away.

3. Privies and water closets shall be constructed within the house or cottage and connected to the sewer.

4. Garbage shall be removed daily.

In 1905, The Monroe Park Association was sold to J. T. M. Johnston and L. S. Parker. The transfer involved 83 lots and 11 cottages including The Florida Beach, Stone Lodge, The Waubeek, Kentucky Home, Rose Bush, Cubby, Sunny Bank, Blue Jay, Bleak House, and two others unnamed. Though the ownership of the north beach area had been with the residents of Monroe Park at one time it was transferred to the City of South Haven.

~Ken and Lynda Hogan 2016

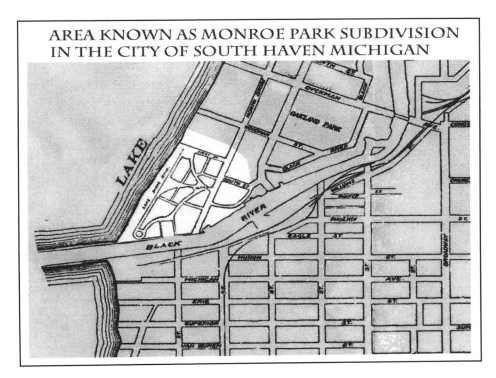

AREA KNOWN AS MONROE PARK SUBDIVISION IN THE CITY OF SOUTH HAVEN MICHIGAN

A Panoramic View

of Monroe Park Subdivison from the North Pier in 1902

The Breakers   The Delmar   Avery Beach Hotel   Keswick   The Grassmere

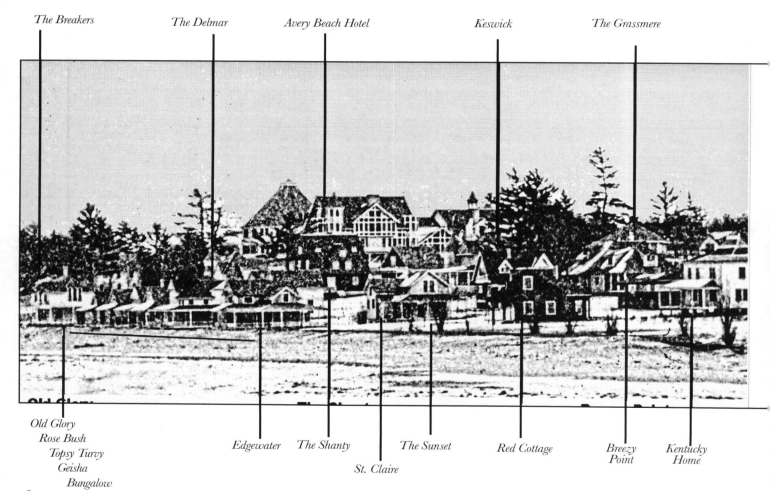

Old Glory
Rose Bush
Topsy Turvy
Geisha
Bungalow

Edgewater   *The Shanty*   *The Sunset*   *Red Cottage*   *Breezy Point*   *Kentucky Home*

St. Claire

Stone Lodge   White Lodge   Oak Park   Florida Beach   Plato   Oak Harbor

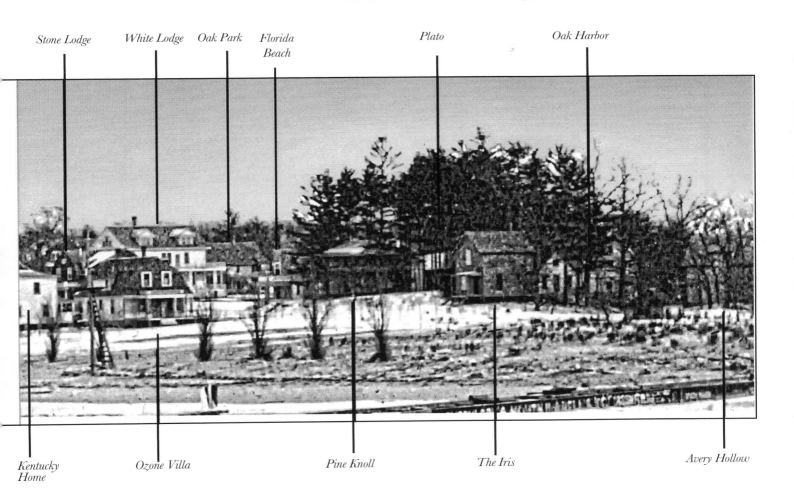

Kentucky Home   Ozone Villa   Pine Knoll   The Iris   Avery Hollow

1920s

27 North Shore Drive

Two lots in the early years

1900 – building named *The Swallows* built

1908-1916 – second building built

1918 – *Monroe Park* and *The Butler* resorts

1925 – *Monroe Park* and *Boika* resorts

1937 – *Fink* and *Bender* resort

1950s – *Appleman Rooms* and *Rubin Rooms*

1960s – one building, 29 North Shore

Drive, demolished

After 1960 the building housed several restaurants, including *Charlie's*, *Huck Finn*, *The Wharf*, and *Channel One*

10

33 North Shore Drive

1899 – Building named *Surprise Rock* converted from a barn; during construction a large rock 7'x 8' on the site was laid bare.

1902 – *The Avery Hollow*

1908-1920 – *The Riverview Resort*

1930s – *Rosenberg Resort*

1950s – *Riverview Resort* and *The Ben Garfinkel Hotel*

1960s – *Richter's Rooms,* demolished

1900

1920s

34 North Shore Drive

1908 – house built

1950s – houses at 34 and 36 become a restaurant called *The Forrest's Lou*

(aerial view) 1960s

1960s

35 North Shore Drive

1890s – house built, called *Plato*

1930s – known as *El Plato*

1960s – known as *The Graise* and *The Graise Beachside Hotel,* demolished in the 1960s

37 North Shore Drive

1890s – cottage built named *The Cubby*

1960s

42 North Shore Drive

1930 – home built for *The Biltmore* owner
1970s-2008 – Became a restaurant named: *Mariner's Inn*,
Rupperts, Three Pelicans, Fish Tales
2008 – demolished

43 North Shore Drive

1930s – *Jack and Jill* duplex and the *Love Nest* were
built as part of *The Florida Beach Hotel*

1979

45 North Shore Drive

1908-1916 – a cottage named *The Jack* was built as part of *The Florida Beach Hotel*

1930s – *The Jack* was added onto and became *The Florida Cafe*

1950s – Portion of the Cafe was removed and the rest returned to a cottage

1920

1930s

1900

50 North Shore Drive

1900 – the resort hotel, *Marsland,* was built

1920 – renamed *The Wayland Hotel*

1930 – renamed *The Biltmore*

1970s – demolished

51 North Shore Drive (now 99 Esplanade)

1880s – the J. B. Upham home became *The White Lodge*

1920s – named *The Annette Resort* before returning to *The White Lodge*

1960s – named *The Sands* and then *The Plantation Restaurant*

1980s – named *The North Beach Inn* and then *Piggozzi's Restaurant*

2008 – demolished

1900

55 North Shore Drive

1900 – named *Tower*

1920s – named *Surf*

1960s – named *Leider Resort*

1900

1980

1900s

56 North Shore Drive

1890s – originally built by L. S. Monroe

1905 – named *The Marsland Annex,* it was moved from 50 North Shore Drive to 56 North Shore Drive

1908 – named *The Kenilworth*

1913 – named *The Whelan*

1930 – it became part of *The Steuben Resort*

1980 – named *The Arundel House*

58 North Shore Drive

1902 – *The Oak Park* built

1908 – named The *Melrose Inn*

1911 – named *The Oak Park Resort*

1920 – named *Steuben Resort*

1930 – a new building erected

1970 – demolished

1911

1930

1930s

63 North Shore Drive

1930s – built and named *Mendelson's Annex*

1970s – demolished

64 North Shore Drive

1880s – *Oakland Cottage* built

1920s – named *The Oakland Resort*

1930-1960s – named *Mendelson's Oakland Resort*

1920

1930

65 North Shore Drive

1912 – *Avery Beach Cottage* moved to this location from 89 North Shore Drive by Mrs. L. J. Lippert

1918 – Mendelson bought the cottage and named it *The Atlantic*

1930 – constructed a new building, *Mendelson's Atlantic Resort*

1970 – demolished

1918

1930s

1880s

1894

69 North Shore Drive

1886 – Averys build *Cottage Vendome*

1894 – expanded the structure and named it *Avery Beach Hotel*

1907 – destroyed by fire

1913-1937 – *The Casino* (pictured on page 23) built and operated

1937 – *The Casino* was destroyed by fire

1937 – *Mendelson's Atlantic Resort* was expanded to include this property; added a motel and a swimming pool

c. 1900

"The Casino," 1930s

1900s

88 Avery Street

1890s – cottage named *The Shanty*

1907 – *The Shanty* destroyed by fire

1927 – new cottage built around this time

1959 – named *Levitt's Resort*

90 Avery Street

1890s – *The Garret* was built

1907 – *The Garret* destroyed by fire

1927 – new cottage built around this time

1959 – named *The Edgewater Resort*

1890s

92 Avery Street

1890s – *The Walton* was built

1907 – *The Walton* was partially destroyed by fire

2012 – Demolished

1935

2000

98 Avery Street

1890s – *The Waubeek* was built

25

92 Chicago Avenue

1902-1908 – sometime between, *Water View* was built

1908 – Life Guard Station moved to south side of Black river; *Water View* probably moved to Chicago Ave about this time

1930s – named *Harbor View*

1890s

date unknown

95 Chicago Avenue

1890s – cottage built

1930s – named *Oak Arbor*

96 Chicago Avenue

1930s – Had the property address of 25 North Shore Drive; named *Harbor Lodge*

1960s – demolished

1970s

1940s

98 Chicago Avenue

1890s – named *The Englewood*

1930s – named *The Bonnie Brae*

100 Chicago Avenue

1890s – named *The French*

1920s – named *The Popular Nook*

1980s

82 Esplanade

1901 – named *The Red Cottage*

1890s

2000

83 Esplanade

1890s – named *The Curtiss;* later, *The Killcare*

1916-1920s – named *The Shack*

84 Esplanade

1916-1927 – cottage built,
named *Fountain Blue*

1960s

86 Esplanade

1901 – named *The Worthington*

1911 – named *The Woodlawn*

1927 – named *The Dorily Lodge*

2000

87 Esplanade

1900 – named *The Keswick*

1906

89 Esplanade

1890s – named *Breezy Point*

1915 – purported to be a "club"
with "ladies of the night" present

1900

95 Esplanade

1916-1927 – building named *The White Lodge Annex*

1970s

1930

10 Grand Boulevard

1908-1916 – cottage built; named *Grande Vista*

1950-1960 – *Finch's Bait Shop* was across
the street

14 Grand Boulevard

1908-1916 – cottage built; named *Laf-A-Lot*

1990 – demolished

1910s

1920s

12 Grand Boulevard

1908-1916 – cottage built; named *Villa Joan*

16 Grand Boulevard

1908-1916 – cottage built; named *The Betmar*

18 Grand Boulevard

1908-1916 – cottage built; named *The Midway Cottage*

2010 – demolished

1930

1920s

20 Grand Boulevard

1908-1916 – cottage built; named *Mt. Vernon*

22 Grand Boulevard

1908-1916 – cottage built; named *Villa Francis*

1960s

1970s

24 Grand Boulevard

1908-1916 – cottage built; named *Villa Torontita*

26, 28 Grand Boulevard

1885 – Life Guard Station erected

1896 – Life Guard Station and *Water View Cottage* before it was moved to 92 Chicago Avenue

1908 – Life Guard Station moved to south side of Black River

1896

1898

27 Grand Boulevard

1908-1916 – cottage was built

1908-1916 – moved to this location
from 33 Promenade

1902 – named *Pleasant View, Wigwam*

1916-1927 – named *The Doll House*

1975

1970s

29, 31, 33, 35 Grand Boulevard

1916-1927 – *Bungalow Court* was built sometime between these dates which
included four cottages named *Never Mind, Cheer Up, Suits Us,* and *Band Box*

29, 31 Grand Boulevard

1916-1927 – two cottages were built sometime between these dates, named *Never Mind* and *Cheer Up*

1920s

1920s

33, 35 Grand Boulevard

1916-1927 –two cottages, *Suits Us* and *Band Box*, were built sometime between these dates

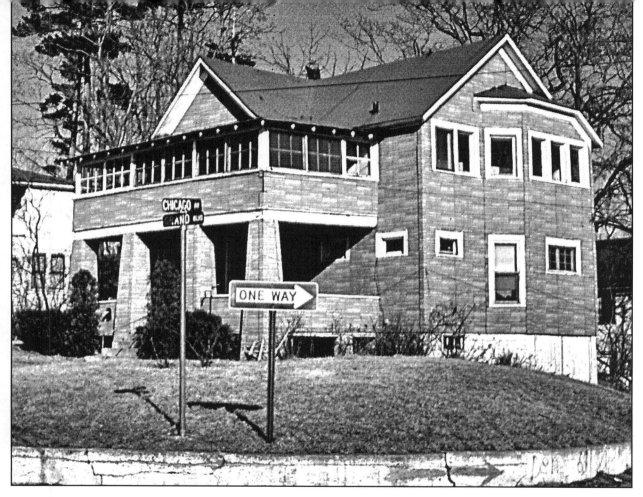

1970s

34 Grand Boulevard

1890s – named *The Iris*

1960s – named *Bank's Rooms*

37 Grand Boulevard

1901 – named *Ozone Villa*

1930s – Sophie Tucker sang there, having pulled
the piano out onto the driveway

1970

38 Grand Boulevard

1910s

1890s – named *Pine Knoll*

1908-1916 – between these dates, cottage was moved to this location from one lot North, 40 Grand; a Michigan basement and boathouse were dug out sometime after it was moved

1940s – rumored to have served briefly as "a brothel"

2000

1970s

1910s – Anna Wagner on beach

40 Grand Boulevard

1901 – named *Shadyside;* originally *Pine Knoll*
was built in front before moving to one lot south

43

1970s

41 Grand Boulevard

1920s – named *Seven Cs*

1927 – named *M & M (Mary May)*

rumored to have a secret hideaway room to avoid police detection

44 & 46 Grand Boulevard

1898 – built by L. S. Monroe, named *Florida*

1906 – named *Rowe's Resort*

1908 – named *The Florida Beach Hotel* which included restaurants featuring Chinese and American menus for several years; Sophie Tucker was said to have sung on the upper porch

1908

1920s

1900

47 Grand Boulevard

1920 – named *H & H* (after Howard Hemsen); later named *Port Oak*

2007 – Demolished

49 Grand Boulevard

1898 – built by L. S. Monroe, named *Stone Lodge*

1927 – operated as a resort for many years

1964 – became a single residence

1970s

1965

53 Kalamazoo

1880 – named The Grasmere

1930s – named The Restaway

49A Grand Boulevard

1930s – was the annex to *Stone Lodge*

1960s – building was moved to Pullman, Michigan, leaving a large yard for Stone Lodge

1906

54 Kalamazoo

1890s – named *Idle Hour*

1950s – named *Sueladon*

1960s – named *Rosenbloom Rooms*

1970

2009

55 Kalamazoo

1916-1927 – cottage built

1940s – named *Sylir*

58 Kalamazoo

1890s – named *The Sills*

1908 – named *The Dixie*

1940 – named *The Hillcrest*

1950-1960 – named *The Sherman Rooms*

2010

2010

60 Kalamazoo

1927 or later – cottage was built

1940s – named *The Rocklin,* and *The Squaw*

2011 – demolished

2010

61 *Kalamazoo*

1890s – named *Bleak House*

62 Kalamazoo

1908-1916 – cottage built

1940s – named *None Such*

2010

2010

63 Kalamazoo

1880s – named *Blue Jay*

1920s – named *Blue Jay*, possibly
Taffy Apple Molly's house

2010

64 Kalamazoo

1908-1916 – cottage built

1940s – named *Bar None*

66 Kalamazoo
(originally 86 Avery)

1890s – named *The Delmar*

1907 – completely destroyed in the *Avery Beach Hotel* fire

1908-1916 – new building erected

1965 – named *The Brenner Cottage*

1890s

1910s

10 Lake Shore Drive

1908-1916 – built sometime between these years

1930s – named *The Ackmoody*

1940s – named *Blue Heaven*

14 Lake Shore Drive

1908-1916 – built sometime between these years,
named *The After Glow*

1920s

18 Lake Shore Drive

1908-1916 – built sometime between these years, named *The Oddity* because of the triangular addition in the rear

2010 – demolished

2010

20 Lake Shore Drive

1908-1916 – built sometime between these years, named *The Villa Framore*

2010

2010

22 Lake Shore Drive

1908-1916 – built between these years, named *The Sandy Nook*

1920s

24 Lake Shore Drive

1908-1911 – built sometime between these years, named *The Bright Lodge*

1920s – named *The Playhouse*

2010

26 Lake Shore Drive

1908-1916 – built sometime between these years, named *The College Inn*

28 Lake Shore Drive

1908-1916 – built sometime between these years, named *Beach View*

1920s

30 Lake Shore Drive

1908-1916 – built sometime between these years, named
The Inverness and then *The Fern*

36 Lake Shore Drive

1908-1916 – built sometime between these years, named *Happy Landing*

2000 – demolished

1970s

2010

36½ Lake Shore Drive

1916-1927 – built sometime between these years

1906

2010

38 Lake Shore Drive

1902-1908 – built sometime between these years, named *The Cement Cottage* because of the siding

1909 – named *The Gray Cottage*, commonly known now as *The Pink House* because of its pink painted exterior

1901

50 Lake Shore Drive

1890s – named *The Sunset*, and *The Sunset Beach Resort*

1940s – named *Grant Camp*

1950s or 1960s – demolished

42 Lake Shore Drive

1901 – named *The Green Cottage*

1930s – named *The Dreamerie*

1950s – named *The Nettie*

1965 – known as *Hunter's Cottage*

2010 – demolished

1890

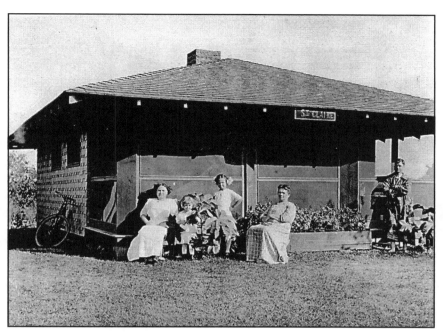

1890s

52 Lake Shore Drive

1890s – named *St. Claire*

54 Lake Shore Drive

1890s – named *The Edgewater*

1920s – named *The Trip Inn*

2010

2010

56 Lake Shore Drive

1902-1908 – built sometime between these years,

named *The Bungalow*

1930s

58 Lake Shore Drive

1890s – named *The Geisha*

1920s – named *Happy Home*

1930 – named *The Sally Anne*

1970s – demolished

2010

2010

60 Lake Shore Drive

1890s – named *Topsy Turvy*

62 Lake Shore Drive

1890s – named *The Rose Bush*

1900

1920

66 Lake Shore Drive

1890s – a cottage named *The Breakers*

1907 – fire started in this cottage which spread rapidly to include seven other cottages and *The Avery Beach Hotel,* everything was a total loss

1908-1916 – new cottage was built sometime between these years

1927 – named *Florette* and *Buddy*

2008 – demolished

2010

64 Lake Shore Drive

1890s – named *Old Glory*

1930s – named *Mary Jean*

1960s – named *Sea Shell*

48 Plaza

1908-1916 – built sometime between these years, named *The Jill* and was part of *The Florida Beach*

1950s – named *The Ronnie* and then *Squeeze Inn*

1960

25 Promenade

1916-1927 – built between these
years, named *The Brownie*

2010

2010

31 Promenade

1916-1927 – built between these years,
named *The Poplar*

33 Promenade

1908-1916 – cottage built

1916-1927 – moved to this location
between these years, named
The Buddy

1940s

KATHRYN·S.

38 Promenade

1916-1927 – built between these years,
named *The Kathryn-S*

1920s

1900s

42 Promenade

1890s – built as a pavilion on Lake Shore Drive *(The Triangle)*

1901 – moved to this location, converted into a two-story house named *Kentucky Home Resort*

2006 – demolished

53 Promenade

1902-1908 – named *The Ariel*

1970s

2010

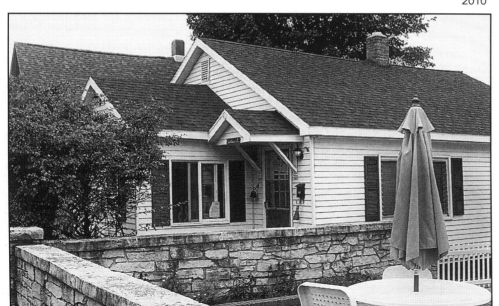

55 Promenade

1927 – built after this year

69

2010

57 Promenade

1890-1902 – built between these years, named *The Wayside*

1920s – named *The Wolverine*

59 Promenade

1890-1902 – built between these years, named *The Olivia*

1920s – named The Carrie Jane

2010

60 Walk B

1890 – named *The Shelter,* north half of the lot had a cottage named *The Sunny Bank* also built in the 1890s but demolished sometime after 1927

1930s

1970s

35 Walk F

1927 – at this location, named *The Tipperary.* The cottage may have been built in 1913 and moved from a lot between 92 & 94 Chicago Ave, about 100 feet to the east; house has a 1913 toilet and a similar design to the design on the 1916 & 1927 Sanborn Insurance map

Appendix

Aerial view of North Beach cottages near the pier, Newcome Resort and Casino in rear, 1920s

Chicago & South Haven Steamship Co.

"The Safest Way"

South Haven?—Yes!

There's Every Reason Why YOU Should Go to South Haven!

A COOL LAKE TRIP— 80 miles of reinvigoration.
  A QUICK Lake Trip— only 4 hours from Chicago.   No Dirt.   No Dust.
    A LUXURIOUS Lake Trip— on the new steel steamer "City of South Haven."

WEEK-END PLEASURING —no time lost from business.
  REUNION WITH THE FAMILY—and at trifling cost.
    GOLF for the Golfer.   TENNIS for the Tennis Player.

AUTOMOBILING on superb roads for the Motorist.
  HORSEBACK RIDING, DRIVING, TRAMPING, SAILING, BOATING.
    BATHING for everybody, from a sloping beach that's safe.

FISHING — in season, in nearby lakes and streams.
  DANCING — in the Pavilions.   SOCIAL PLEASURE everywhere.
    FRUIT FARMING for those who would make pleasure profitable.

WHOLESOME COUNTRY FARE and keen appetite for it.
  PURE ARTESIAN WATER.   PURE AIR.   IDEAL SURROUNDINGS.
    THE COMFORTS OF HOME in the atmosphere of a Resort.

IN A WORD, South Haven is a Family Resort, patronized by
  the best people — a resort that provides amusement for every member of the family —
  a resort where parents feel safe in
  bringing their children.

STERILIZED AND FILTERED WATER USED EXCLUSIVELY

Travel brochure, 1916

AVERY BEACH RESORT: 8 COTTAGES BURNED

THE EARLY MORNING FIRE CAUSES LOSS OF $125,000 IN HEART OF RESORT COLONY

Flames, Starting at "The Breakers" Swept by Gale, From Lake to North Shore Drive

Comparatively Little Property Saved

Newspaper, 1907

L. S. Monroe residence, 125 North Shore Drive, 1900

Steamship advertisement, 1900

"THERE'S ONLY ONE SOUTH HAVEN"

"There's only one South Haven"
It's on Lake Michigan's Shore,
Such fishing and such boating
Were never known before.

"There's only one South Haven"
Where the sunset's azure hues
Makes one feel life's worth living,
And drives away the blues.

"There's only one South Haven"
So the tens of thousands say,
Who come here every Summer
To pass the time away.

All o'er our country wide
You'll hear these thousands say
"There's only one South Haven,
If only for a day."

Postcard, 1905

Promotional brochure, 1900

... THE DINING ROOM. ...

EXTENDS the entire front of the east wing, faced with a broad veranda, overlooking the play ground and grove. The main entrance is from the Rotunda with its splendid lake view.

... BATHING. ...

NO finer Beach can be found for safe Bathing. The Management have made arrangements at considerable expense with the Beach Bath House Co. to give those guests who want to indulge in lake bathing, rooms. Towels will be furnished and an attendant will take charge of bathing.

Avery Beach Resort.

SOUTH HAVEN, Michigan, May 10, 1897.

THE advantages of South Haven as a summer home becoming more generally known, there is every prospect of a much earlier opening of the season than usual. To meet this we will open our Dining Room, and a portion of our Hotel on June 1st to take care of early arrivals.

Letters of inquiry may be sent to Avery Beach Resort, South Haven, as early as June 1st, or to the Chicago office as per page 3 in booklet.

The Avery Beach Company make use of a private sewer of over one-half mile in length, substantially built—the only Resort Hotel here that is thus sewered, and has on each of its floors fine toilet rooms with perfect plumbing attachments.

Address until June 17th, ...

Avery Beach Resort,
Room 81, 147 Fifth Avenue,

Per week each ... two persons, $8.00 $9.00 $10.00 ... 7.00 8.00 ... 8.00 to 10.00 ...

Our Hotel Coach for the free transfer of Guests will meet trains and steamers.

The agents of the Rushmore Transfer Company will be at Depots and Steamer Landings, and give checks for Trunks and be responsible for safe delivery at 25c each.

Address after June 17th, ...

Avery Beach Resort,
South Haven, Michigan

Promotional brochure, 1904

Sheet Music, 1926

Newspaper advertisement, 1944

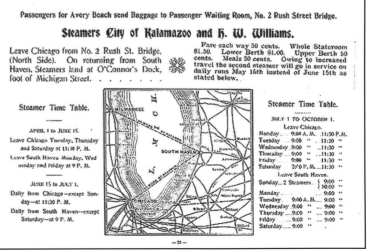

Steamship advertisement, 1900

Promotional brochure, 1920

Newspaper article, 1898

Newspaper advertisement, 1905

THE SOUTH HAVEN OF TODAY   11

Here amidst these natural resources on
the East shore of Lake Michigan where
auto drives unsurpassed abound. Come and
build thy more stately summer mansion,
knowing that the delightful charms here
presented will become more endearing as
season after season you anticipate the
opening of your country home.

South Haven is well prepared to min-
ister to the needs and wants of the count-
less thousands, who visit here for a few
days, a few weeks or longer, that floating
population who find here, during their
brief stay, away from business cares, the
unsurpassing hospitality of well managed
hotels and resorts, making them welcome
and at ease. To care for this ever increasing population there are more than a
hundred places of entertainment in and
around the city where from a score to as
many as five hundred people are lodged,
fed and made welcome.

The forms of amusement are so many
and so varied that regardless of what your
own particular preferences may be,
you will not be disappointed. Here at
this ideal resort of the inland seas, where
the cool refreshing water makes the hot
blasts of summer unknown, the gentle
breezes and sweet perfumed air of Michigan awaits you.

Promotional brochure

ALL OCCUPIED NOW

Unusual Record Before August First; Resorts Also Report Large Crowds

For the first time in the history of Monroe Park, every cottage in it is occupied before the first of August. One or two of the cottages that are now occupied by the owners are for rent for the remainder of the season. but unless they can be rented at good figures, the owners will remain in them thruout the season.

This unusual condition is of more than ordinary interest and importance because of a few calamity yowls that have gone up that, "there is nobody here." Not only are the cottages and larger homes in the resort district taken, but nearly all of the resorts are full or nearly so, and have reservations that insure full houses thru August and well into September.

Newspaper article, 1910

- ALL GUESTS LEAVING MUST BE CHECKED OUT BY 2 P.M. DAY OF DEPARTURE.

NOT RESPONSIBLE FOR ANY ARTICLES LOST OR MISSING.

STONE LODGE RESORT

Rental notice card, 1930

ADVANCE SALE.

Summer Corsets
Summer Underwear
Summer Hosiery

We have bought a large quantity of these goods in order to get them at the lowest figure and can afford to sell a large part of them at about cost, which we shall do at this advance sale. Think of it—new fresh goods at about one-half the regular price.

Having received a large consignment of Summer Corsets—much more than we can sell during the summer season—we wish to sell at least **one-half** of this lot in advance of the regular season and in order to ac- complish this we will sell Corsets which usually sell for 45 and 50 cents at the low price of

25c.

Come early and get the benefit of this reduction. An opportunity to be prepared in advance of the season and at reduced prices. The surplus must be sold NOW in order that we may dispose of our entire stock during the season.

SUMMER UNDERWEAR

A full assortment just arrived. These too will be offered at our Ad- vance sale for prices much below the regular rates.

SUMMER HOSIERY

A Fine line of "Fast Black" and colors especially made for us.

TAN
CHOCOLATE
OX BLOOD

The correct colors for the coming season.

3 pair for $1.00

M. Hale & Company.

Newspaper advertisement, 1897

Steamship brochure, 1916

Kalamazoo, Mich., June 7, '99.

W. Elkenburg,

    South Haven, Mich.

Dear Sir:—I am more than ever anxious to dispose of my North side cottage. Will you kindly reduce the price from $950 to $850 and see if any of the people in and around your vacinity know a good thing when they see it.

       Yours at a loss.

W. ELKENBURG,

Real Estate and Insurance,

Town Hall Building,
South Haven,   Michigan.

P. S.—A fine home, nicely furnished, for rent for the summer months.

Newspaper advertisement 1899

Steamship brochure, 1916

IN SOUTH HAVEN — IT'S

MENDELSON'S ATLANTIC KOSHER HOTEL

ON THE LAKE

Everybody's welcome — Rooms with private bath. Fishing Pier, Private Beach, Casino, Tennis, Shuffleboard and all Summer Sports.

Write for full information and make your reservations early

D. MENDELSON ATLANTIC RESORT

65 North Shore Drive   Phone 511

South Haven, Michigan

Newspaper advertisement, 1940

2,000 Visitors.

We have taken some pains to learn about how many resorters were in town on Sunday last, July 31st. Of course we have been able to reach only those easiest of access, which figured up about 1,400, to which must be added the private cottagers at Monroe Park and elsewhere, which we think makes the estimate of 2,000 a very conservative one.

Newspaper article, 1910

RUDDER STATION.

THE COOLEST PLACE IN SOUTH HAVEN.

=== THE ===

MIDWAY

LESTER W. NEWBRE,
Proprietor.

Row Boats, Canoes and Launches.

Rapid Ferry Boats. The Best Service on the River.

Launches for all the
          Points Up Black River.

Launches can be Chartered for Special Trips,
Moonlight or Fishing Excursions.

DOCKS AND BOATHOUSE,

On River Below Hotel Marsland.

Handbill, 1890-1920

The Latest Fad for the Seashore
25c   Cork Balls   25c

Gives amusement to old and young. Weighs but one and one-half ounces. Organize your Water Polo Teams.

Porch Swings

"Two is company, three is a crowd." This swing is large enough to seat two comfortably and strong enough to hold four.

Our bargain price **$3**

Hammocks

A good serviceable Hammock   **$1.35**

All $5.00 Vudor Reinforced Hammocks $2.00

Newspaper advertisement, 1912

Location Map
Street Address Number with Page Number

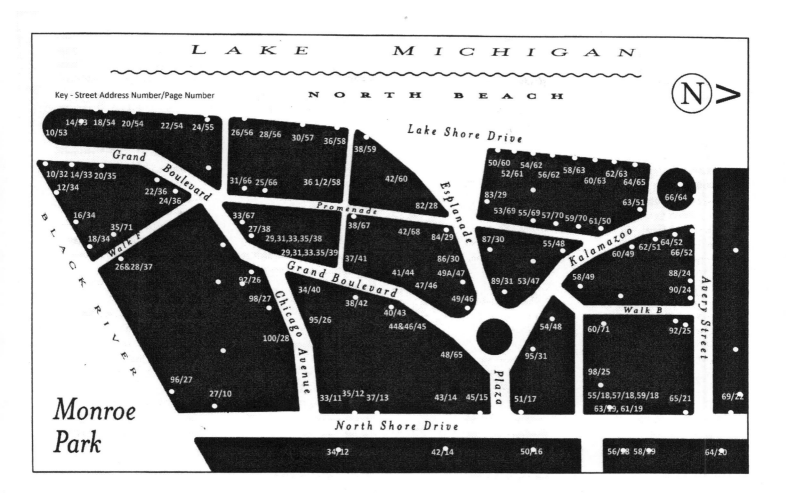

LAKE MICHIGAN

NORTH BEACH

N >

Key - Street Address Number/Page Number

Lake Shore Drive

14/53 18/54 20/54 22/54 24/55
10/53

26/56 28/56 30/57 36/58
38/59

50/60 54/62 58/63 62/63
52/61 56/62 60/63 64/65

66/64

Grand Boulevard

10/32 14/33 20/35
12/34

22/36
24/36

31/66 25/66 36 1/2/58

42/60

83/29

63/51

16/34

35/71

Promenade

82/28

53/69 55/69 57/70 59/70 61/50

18/34

Walk F

33/67

38/67

42/68

84/29

87/30

55/48

62/51 64/52
60/49 66/52

26&28/37

27/38
29,31,33,35/38
29,31,33.35/39

37/41

86/30

89/31 53/47

58/49

88/24
90/24

BLACK RIVER

92/26

Grand Boulevard

41/44

49A/47
47/46

49/46

Walk B

98/27

34/40

38/42

60/71

92/25

Chicago Avenue

95/26

40/43
44&46/45

54/48

95/31

98/25

100/28

48/65

Plaza

51/17

55/18,57/18,59/18
63/19, 61/19

65/21

69/22

96/27

27/10

33/11 35/12 37/13

43/14 45/15

Monroe
Park

North Shore Drive

34/12

42/14

50/16

56/18 58/19

64/20

Esplanade

Kalamazoo

Avery Street

Index

Acknowledgements

Photo Credits

R. W. Appleyard

Sheila Biederman

Henry Barber

Donna and Ron Goodrich

Bob and Kay Hemsen

Lynda and Ken Hogan

Charlene Klein

Earl Novak

Helen B. O'Rourke

South Haven Historical Association

South Haven Maritime Museum

South Haven Memorial Library

Don Schultz

Roland Springate

Leslie Rolle Weber

Special Thanks

Ed Appleyard

Susan Hale

Jim Ollgaard

Book Design and Production

David Dumo

Roberta Richardson

Made in the USA
Middletown, DE
12 July 2018